THE FROGS WHO WANTED A KING

THE FROGS WHO WANTED A KING
and other songs from *La Fontaine*

collected by EDWARD SMITH

illustrated by MARGOT ZEMACH

FOUR WINDS PRESS

NEW YORK

Library of Congress Cataloging in Publication Data

The Frogs who wanted a king, and other songs from La Fontaine.

French and English.
Summary: The fables of La Fontaine set to music, with words in French and English.
1. Children's songs. 2. Children's songs, French.
3. La Fontaine, Jean de, 1621–1695—Musical settings.
[1. Songs, French. 2. La Fontaine, Jean de, 1621–1695—Musical settings]
I. Smith, Edward, harpsichordist.
II. La Fontaine, Jean de, 1621–1695. Fables. English and French. 1977.
III. Zemach, Margot.
M1997.F928 [M1619.5.L23] 784.6'24 77–5819
ISBN 0–590–17294–8

Music transcription by Maxwell Weaner
Book design by Lucy Martin Bitzer

Published by Four Winds Press
A Division of Scholastic Magazines, Inc., New York, N.Y.
Text copyright © 1977 by Edward Smith
Illustrations copyright © 1977 Margot Zemach
Printed in the United States of America
Library of Congress Catalog Card Number: 77–5819

1   2   3   4   5   81 80 79 78 77

Contents

Introduction

The present collection of Fables is a rare example of eighteenth-century music intended expressly for children. Most of the lyrics were adapted directly from the celebrated Fables of Jean de La Fontaine: for the most part, they have been fitted to the tunes with admirable skill. Those readers who may miss the wit and elegance of La Fontaine's verse we hope will be appeased by the charm of the musical settings. In some cases, the fable is referred to only obliquely, the assumption being that French children would already be familiar with La Fontaine's work. These versions are simplifications only in the sense that the tunes require the original poems to be fitted into a concise and limited rhythmic pattern. Eighteenth-century children were dressed (and treated) like miniature adults, and these fables are every bit as sophisticated as the similar parodies of popular airs which were circulated among the grown-ups.

It is unlikely that La Fontaine would have approved of these latter-day versions of his fables. Although he dedicated two of his collections to royal children, he refused to limit himself ("... mon humeur n'étant nullement de m'arrêter à ce petit peuple," he remarked), and he clearly intended his verses to be savored by fully mature readers.

Beginning with Aesop, from whom La Fontaine took the bulk of his subject matter, fables have been enjoyed by both young and old for their colorful and pithy folk wisdom and their acute observation of animal and human character and behavior. No one has offered a better definition than La Fontaine himself in the preface to his first book of fables: "... ces fables sont un tableau où chacun de nous se trouve dépeint. Ce qu'elles présentent confirme les personnes d'âge avancé dans les connaissances que l'usage leur a donnés, et apprend aux enfants ce qu'il faut qu'ils sachent. Comme ces derniers sont nouveau-venues dans le monde, ils n'en connaissent pas encore les habitants, ils ne se connaissent pas eux-mêmes. On ne les doit laisser dans cette ignorance que le moins qu'on peut; il leur faut apprendre ce que c'est un lion, un renard, ainsi du reste; et pourquoi l'on compare quelquefois un homme à ce renard ou à ce lion. C'est à quoi les fables travaillent; les premières notions de ces choses proviennent d'elles."[1] And here is his definition in verse:

> Les fables ne sont pas ce qu'elles semblent être.
> Le plus simple animal nous y tient lieu de maître.
> Une morale nue apporte de l'ennui:
> Le conte fait passer le précepte avec lui.
> En ces sorte de feinte il faut instruire et plaire,
> Et conter pour conter me semble peu d'affaire.[2]

"Instruire et plaire" are goals of all good education; and this desire is echoed in the preface to our collection. Referring to the children for whom their book was intended, the compilers add hopefully, "On s'es-timera heureux si en leur donnant de l'attrait pour des leçons utiles et qui conviennent à leur âge, on pourrait les dégoûter de tant de chansons profanes qu'on leur met dans la bouche, et qui ne serve qu'à corrompre leur innocence."[3]

Of the various titles of the several editions in which this collection appeared, the fullest is: *Fables Choisies dans le gout de M. de la Fontaine, sur des Vaudevilles et petits Airs aisés à chanter, avec leur Basse et une Basse en Musette.* It first appeared in 1730 as a supplement to a collection of devotional songs, *Nouvelles Poésies Spirituelles et Morales sur les plus beaux Airs de la Musique Française et Italienne.* At least six editions followed over a span of some twenty years, attesting to the work's popularity. (The Fables were also offered in a separate smaller format, with the unharmonized tunes printed in an appendix.)

No authors are mentioned by the publishers or booksellers Desprez, Desessarts, Lottin or Guichard, whose names appear on the title page of the first edition. Subsequent volumes include only the laconic remark, "The basses have been figured with great care by M. Clérambault, for the convenience of those who accompany at the harpsichord, or with theorbo." Louis-Nicolas Clérambault (1676–1749), director of music for Mme. de Maintenon at Saint-Cyr, and organist at Saint Sulpice in Paris, was the celebrated composer of several books of cantatas that were held in great esteem as models of the genre. His skill is evident in the elegant harmonizations of these tunes; no doubt it was he who added the basses and the ornament signs as well.

The tunes themselves represent only a few of the many hundreds which circulated during the *ancien régime* under the names *vaudeville*, *brunette*, *air à boire* and *musette*, among others. They were endlessly adapted to new words, in turn satirical, pastoral or licentious. (A familiar example of this practice is *The Beggar's Opera*.) Rarely did these tunes acquire the high moral tone exhibited in our collection of fables. The original edition identifies each melody by its best-known title. Such subjects as *Dans notre Village, Ah! ma commère es-tu fachée?, Tique tique tac et lon lan l*à and *Ce Charmant vin de Champagne* are characteristic.[4]

The editor examined copies of the Fables in the Library of the Performing Arts, Lincoln Center, New York City, and in the Bibliothèque Nationale in Paris; the cooperation of their respective staffs is gratefully acknowledged. While this is obviously not intended to be a scholarly edition, editorial interference with the original text has been kept to a minimum. Where indicated, the songs have been transposed to bring them within the range of young voices;[5] spelling, clefs and time signatures have been modernized; and keyboard accompaniments have been added. These harmonizations have been kept as simple as possible for the benefit of those with modest keyboard skills; players able to produce more elaborate versions may use the original figured bass as a guide.

These songs embody that blend of naïveté and sophistication so dear to eighteenth-century taste. The predominance of one or the other in performance will depend upon one's skill and taste. It is unlikely that many children (or adults either, for that matter) will be able to manage the vocal ornaments scattered so generously throughout these pieces. (Could eighteenth-century children really sing trills?) Some of them at least should be attempted, since ornamentation is such an integral part of this music.

The original editions include a *basse en musette* (drone bass on the tonic, in imitation of the bagpipe); these were added, explains the preface, especially for children, "making it very easy for them to play on the harpsichord, or any other instrument." This could include any keyboard instrument, cello, viol, guitar, or whatever happens to be at hand. The manner of performance should be limited only by one's musical imagination. Any of the Fables may be sung (with or without accompaniment) as a duet or two-part chorus, since the bass line was especially designed to fit the rhythm of the words. The drone may be substituted for the bass, with the appropriate harmonies played over this by the keyboard player's right hand, or by whatever accompanying instrument is being used; or a simple drone pattern of octaves and fifths may be employed. Each verse of a song might be treated in a different way; and the animals themselves can be characterized by different sorts of accompaniment.[6]

In conclusion, the editor shares the hope expressed by De Lalande, Superintendent of the King's Music, in giving official approval to the book: "Les Fables sont autant d'utiles leçons, que la charme de la voix en flattant l'oreille pourra agréablement faire passer jusqu'au coeur."[7]

Notes

1. "These fables are a picture in which each of us is represented. Their content confirms what experience has taught mature adults, and teaches children what they must learn. As the young are newcomers to the world, they do not yet know its inhabitants, nor do they know themselves. They should not remain in this ignorance any longer than is necessary. They must be taught what a lion is, what a fox is, and so on; and why a man is sometimes compared to the fox or lion. This is the fable's purpose; our first encounters with such matters come from them."

2. Fables are not what they seem to be;
    The humblest creature can make us see.
    An unclothed moral is boring at best:
    A story well-told makes us swallow the rest.
    A fable should please as it teaches, you see,
    For a tale with no moral means nothing to me.

3. "We will be most gratified if, by attracting them to useful lessons suitable to their age, we may turn them away from all those worldly songs that adults put into their mouths, and which only serve to corrupt their innocence."

4. Parodists did not always limit themselves to popular tunes; they sometimes appropriated works of famous composers. See page 16 in this edition, which is set to François Couperin's *La Pastorelle*. (Couperin himself left two versions of this: a song, and a harpsichord piece.)

5. In most cases, the transposed key will be the pitch level at which the song would have been sung in eighteenth-century France, i.e., a half- or whole-step lower than our present-day pitch.

6. See page 53 for a suggested version of one of the Fables.

To an eighteenth-century singer, ornamentation was as necessary to music as were imagery, metaphor and figures of speech to rhetoric; ornaments gave force, brilliance and color to the words they decorated. They should never be mechanical or merely "correct."

In his treatise of 1755, *L'Art du Chant*, Jean Baptiste Bérard gives no fewer than twelve ornaments which he considers necessary to good singing. As we see in our collection of Fables, these ornaments were indicated by only two signs: ⟋⟍ always means a trill, while + can also mean trill, as well as a variety of other ornaments. It was up to the singer to know which ornament was appropriate at a given spot.

A few basic ornaments are illustrated below. It is important to note the context of the ornamented note, whether it is approached from above or from below. It will be seen that, in general, trills are appropriate in a descending line, and mordents in an ascending one.

Tremblement (trill)

Pincé (mordent)

Port de voix en ascendent (appoggiatura from below)

Port de voix et pincé

Port de voix en descendent (appoggiatura from above)

Double (turn)

7. "The Fables are useful lessons which the voice's charm, as it flatters the ear, may agreeably carry to the heart."

Le Corbeau et le Renard
La flaterie

Légèrement

I Un cor-beau te-nant un fro-ma-ge, Au haut d'un arbre é-
II Le ru-sé lui tint ce lan-ga-ge: Peut-on voir plus gen-

ORIGINAL KEY: d

tait per-ché: Re-nard é-tait au voi-si-na-ge, Et par l'o-deur fut al-lé-ché.
til oi-seau? Si la voix ré-pond au plu-ma-ge, Le mon-de n'a rien de plus beau.

[3]
De plaisir l'oiseau noir croasse;
Le morceau lui tombe du bec.
Le renard vite le remasse,
Et dit: Je vais souper avec.

[4]
Apprenez, poursuit-il, beau sire,
Qu'on ne vous flatte point pour rien:
L'adulateur ne vous admire,
Que pour escroquer votre bien.

THE CROW AND THE FOX
Flattery

[1] Holding cheese in his beak, a crow was perched high in a tree. Renard the fox was near by, and was attracted by the smell.

[2] The sly fellow said to the crow, "Could one hope to see a lovelier bird than you? If your voice matches your plumage, there can be nothing more beautiful in all the world!"

[3] As the bird croaked with pleasure, the cheese fell from his beak. The fox quickly seized it and said, "I'll have this for supper.

[4] "You must learn, milord," he added, "no one flatters you for nothing. The flatterer praises you to steal your possessions."

Le Pot de Terre et le Pot de Fer
La témérité

Rondement et marqué

I Aux ris-ques de l'o-ra-ge Pour-quoi vous ex-po-ser? Si vous fai-tes nau-

THE CLAY POT AND THE IRON POT
Recklessness

Why expose yourself to the dangers of a storm? If you are shipwrecked, who would say you're not to blame? A fragile pot of clay bumped into an iron pot. When it was smashed to bits, people said that the reckless thing deserved it.

3

Le Chien Qui Se Voit dans l'Eau
L'ombre pour le corps

Marqué

I L'on - de trans - pa - ren - te   Au chien re - pré - sen - te   Le fri - and mor - ceau Qu'il te - nait au   mu - seau.

II Pour une es - pé - ren - ce,   Pour une ap - pa - ren - ce,   La cu - pi - di - té   Perd la ré - a - li - té.

ORIGINAL KEY: g   6   7   6   6   6   4

4

THE DOG WHO SEES HIS REFLECTION IN THE WATER
The shadow for the substance

[1] The clear pool shows the dog the tasty morsel he holds in his mouth. When he drops his bone to dive into the water, another dog grabs it. (That's the best part.) And the shepherd sings with merry voice, "The clear pool shows the dog the tasty morsel he holds in his mouth."

[2] For a mere hope, for an illusion, a greedy person loses the real thing. This is the sickness of the human race, that sacrifices everything for vanity, and is reprimanded in vain for its folly: for a mere hope, for an illusion, a greedy person loses the real thing.

Le Lion et le Rat

L'humanité

Gaiment

I Un rat se trou-va, dit-on, Sous les pat-tes d'un li-
II Quel-que peu de jours a-près, Le li-on fut pris aux

on. on. Le fier a-ni-mal, Sans lui fai-re mal, Loin d'en-trer en fu-ri-
rets: rets: A-lors no-tre rat Ne fut point in-grat, Ni de pe-tit u-sa-

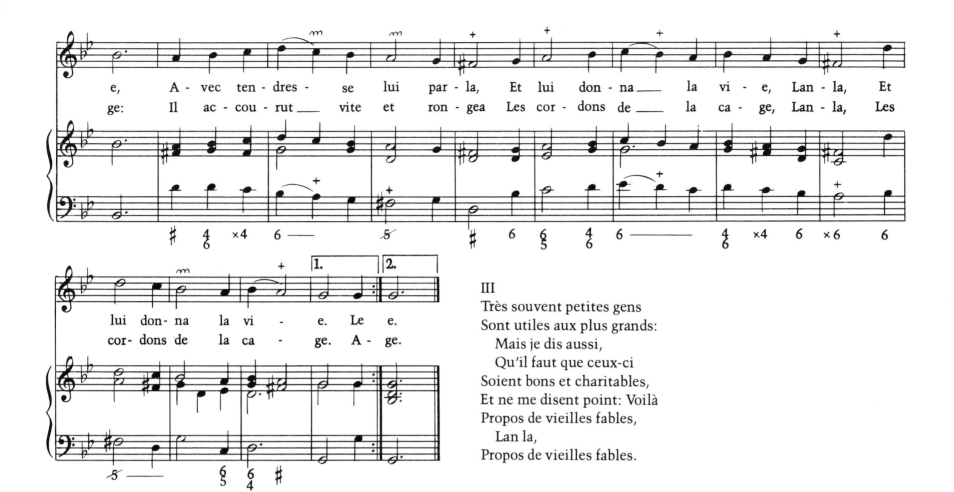

e,   A- vec ten- dres- se lui par- la,   Et lui don- na___ la vi- e,   Lan - la,   Et
ge: Il ac- cou- rut ___ vite et ron- gea   Les cor- dons de ___ la ca- ge,   Lan - la,   Les

lui don- na   la vi -   e. Le   e.
cor- dons de   la ca -   ge. A-   ge.

III

Très souvent petites gens
Sont utiles aux plus grands:
    Mais je dis aussi,
    Qu'il faut que ceux-ci
Soient bons et charitables,
Et ne me disent point: Voilà
Propos de vieilles fables,
    Lan la,
Propos de vieilles fables.

THE LION AND THE RAT
"Human" kindness

[1] A rat, it is said, was once stepped on by a lion. The proud animal did not harm him, and instead of being angry, spoke to him gently and spared his life.

[2] A few days later the lion was caught in a net. Then our rat, who was neither ungrateful nor ill-mannered, quickly ran up and gnawed the ropes of the snare.

[3] Very often little folk prove useful to the great. But I may add that these important people should be good and charitable; nor should they say, "That's just stuff in old fables, la la, stuff in old fables."

Les Deux Chiens et Leur Maître

L'éducation

Légèrement

ORIGINAL KEY: g

I Un per-son-na-ge de re-nom,
II Cet homme a-vait un au-tre chien,

Gen-til-homme et ri-che, dit-on,
Moins ché-rit, quoi-que chas-sant bien,

En-tre-te-nait un chien mi-gnon,
Et ne man-quant ja-mais en rien,

III

Mais du gibier qu'on apprêtait,
Chien chasseur jamais ne tâtait:
Et chien oisif s'en ragoûtait
   A la table du maître,
Dans le temps qu'à l'autre on jettait
   Pain bis par la fenêtre.

IV

Pour ce bélître que voilà
   Sans chômer je travaille:
Et lui seul se dorlotant là,
   Par mes soins fait ripaille.

V

Roger Bontemps qui l'entendit,
   Sans rancune lui répondit:
C'est notre maître qui vous fit
   A la fatigue austère,
Et qui, sage ou non, ne m'apprit
   Qu'à manger sans rien faire.

THE TWO DOGS AND THEIR MASTER
Education

[1] A person of renown who was both noble and rich (it is said) had a pretty little dog. It was idle and good for nothing; its only accomplishment was going around town with its master.

[2] This man had another dog, less esteemed, although he hunted well and never could be faulted either for his spirit or skill, so much so that through his efforts there was an unending supply of game.

[3] But the hunting dog never got to touch the game that was prepared. The lazy dog ate his fill at his master's table, while the other was thrown black bread from the window.

[4] Very unhappy with this state of affairs, he said: "What is this? For that piece of fluff I work without stopping, yet he alone, indulging himself there, benefits from my labors!"

Fai - né - ant, in - u - ti - le, Et sa - chant pour tou - te le - con
Ni d'ar - deur ni d'a - dres - se, Tel - le - ment que par son moy - en

L'ac - com - pa - gner en _____ vil - - le.
Gi - bier ve - nait sans _____ ces - - se.

VI

Quand on reproche aux jeunes gens
    D'être ignares et fainéants,
Visiblement à leurs parents
    La satire s'adresse.
Que veut-on que soient des enfants
    Qu'on n'instruit ni ne dresse?

VII

La fable encore nous apprend
Que les grands services qu'on rend
Ne sont payés le plus souvent
    Que d'un mince salaire;
Et qu'on gagne communement
Moins à servir qu'à plaire.

[5] Hearing this, Froufrou unspitefully replied, "It's our master who gave you your hard tasks, and, wisely or not, he taught me only to eat and do nothing."

[6] When children are reproached for being ignorant and idle, it is their parents who are really being criticized. How do people think children should act, if they're not educated and trained?

[7] This fable also shows us that, more often than not, great services are rewarded by a small recompence; and that usually less is earned by working than by pleasing.

9

La Mouche et la Fourmi

Sotte vanité

ORIGINAL KEY: G

I Je suis, di - sait la mou - che, A la ta - ble des rois: Dans leur pa - lais je cou - che, Et mê - me quel - que - fois Je per - che sur leur nez, j'y dan - se, je m'y jou - e. D'un pe - tit air mig -

II Pour toi, ché - tif in - sec - te, Dit - elle à la four - mi, Dans ta de - meure ab - jec - te Tu ne vis qu'à de - mi: A pei - ne les bour - geois te don - nent quelque en - tré - e Dans le coin d'un sil -

non, Don don, Tan - tôt ci, tan - tôt là, La la, Je les pince à la jou - e.
lon, Don don, Loin de ces mes - sieurs là, La la, L'on te voit en - ter - ré - e.

III
Oui, dit la ménagère:
Mais je suis en repos,
Sans froid et sans misère,
Sans aucun de tes maux:
Et quant à tes beaux jeux (bien sot
    qui les envie)
Même avec la guenon, Don don,
Jouant comme cela, La la,
N'y perds-tu pas la vie?

IV
Plusieurs par le frivole
Se vantent d'être heureux:
Et dans leur tête folle,
Tout est au dessous d'eux.
Laissons-les à leur gré se bercer
    dans le vide:
Ni le beau ni le bon, Don don,
Jamais ne se trouva, La la,
Sinon dans le solide.

THE FLY AND THE ANT
Foolish pride

[1] "I always eat at the king's table," said the fly. "I sleep in his palace, and sometimes I even perch right on the royal noses to dance and frolic. To a pretty little tune, now here, now there, I bite them on the cheeks.

[2] "As for you, you miserable little bug," she said to the ant, "you're only half alive in your wretched hut: as soon as some commoner leaves his door open, you go off and bury yourself in a pile of dirt."

[3] "That may be," replied the little housewife, "but my life is peaceful; and I avoid cold and hardship, and all of your worries. And as for your clever games, only a fool would envy them. Even playing your tricks with a monkey could cost you your life, couldn't it?"

[4] There are many who equate frivolity with happiness, and in their silly heads, all else is beneath them. Let them lull themselves in their vacuum—beauty and goodness will never be found there: they exist only in what is solid and real.

Le Rat et l'Eléphant
Sotte vanité

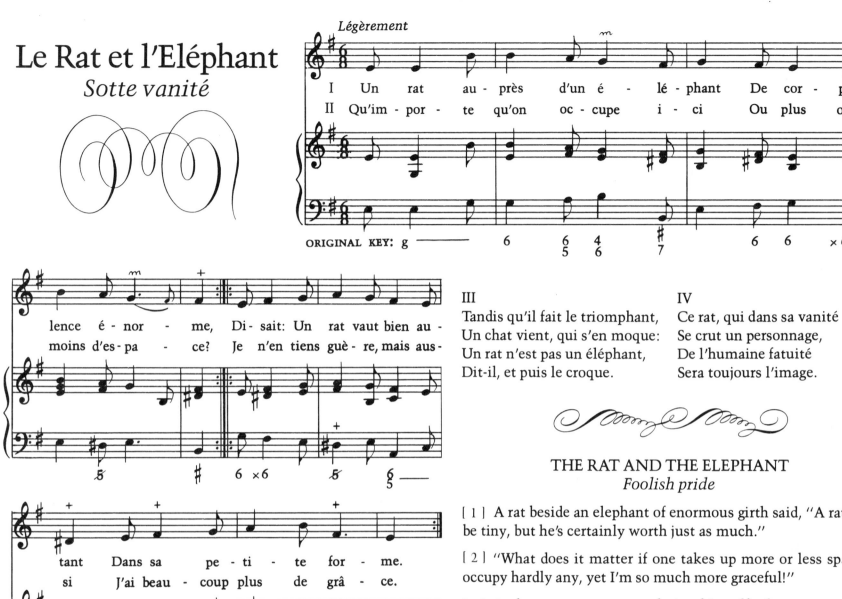

ORIGINAL KEY: g

III

Tandis qu'il fait le triomphant,
Un chat vient, qui s'en moque:
Un rat n'est pas un éléphant,
Dit-il, et puis le croque.

IV

Ce rat, qui dans sa vanité
Se crut un personnage,
De l'humaine fatuité
Sera toujours l'image.

THE RAT AND THE ELEPHANT
Foolish pride

[1] A rat beside an elephant of enormous girth said, "A rat may be tiny, but he's certainly worth just as much."

[2] "What does it matter if one takes up more or less space? I occupy hardly any, yet I'm so much more graceful!"

[3] As he went on congratulating himself, along came a cat, who was not impressed. "A rat is no elephant," said he, and gobbled him up.

[4] This rat whose vanity deceived him into thinking himself important, is an eternal image of human conceit.

La Poule
aux Oeufs d'Or
L'avidité

Légèrement et marqué

I   U - ne pou - le qui pon - dait, Un oeuf d'or cha-
II Ce n'é - tait qu'un i - di - ot, Et le plus sot

que jour - né - e, A son maî - tre ré - pon - dait D'un tré - sor pour chaque an - né -
de la fou - le, En di - sant: J'ai le gros lot Dans la pan - se de ma pou -

e; Mais par un ca - price im - per - ti - nent Il vou - lut a - voir in - con - ti-
le. Il la prit sou - dain et l'é - ven - tra, Et pas un brin d'or n'y ren - con-

nent En main tou - te la som -
tra; On la mit au po - ta -

me, Et se crut un ha-bile hom - me.
ge. Pon- dit- el - le da - van - ta - ge?

THE HEN WHO LAID GOLDEN EGGS
Greed

[1] A hen who laid a golden egg each day provided a yearly treasure for her master; but yielding to a foolish caprice, he couldn't resist wanting the whole amount in his hands at once (and he thought himself an intelligent person)!

[2] He was but a fool among a crowd of fools when he said, "Here I have the whole treasure in the belly of my hen." He suddenly picked her up and cut her open, but not a grain of gold did he find. She was made into soup; and do you think she laid any more golden eggs?

Le Lièvre et les Grenouilles
Le poltron

Légèrement

I Ah! S'é-cri- ait un lièvre au gî- te, Ah! que la peur rend___ mal-heu-reux: Un rien a-gi-te, Et dans la

II C'é-tait pour tant bruit de zé-phi-re: Et l'a-ni-mal voit___ son er-reur; Mais sans mot di- re, Aux champs il

fui- te Se sauve à pei-ne_____ le peu-reux. Mais fu-yons

ti- re, Et sur ses pas croit___ le chas-seur. On a beau

vi- te: De ma gué-ri- te J'en-tends son-ner un___ cor ou deux!

li- re, Voir et s'in-strui- re; On ne gué-rit point___ de la peur.

III

Notre poltron dans son voyage
Trouve poltrons plus grands encore:
    A son passage
    Un marécage
Offre grenouilles sur son bord:
    La gent sauvage
    Vite à la nage
Vers son asile prend l'essor.

IV

Eh! quoi! l'on fuit lorsque je passe,
Dit le coureur. Qu'est donc ceci?
    Prenons de grâce
    Un peu d'audace:
Mais il faudrait du coeur aussi;
    Et notre race,
    Quoi qu'elle fasse,
N'aura jamais qu'un coeur transi.

16

THE HARE AND THE FROGS
The coward

[1] "Ah," cried a hare in his hideaway, "ah, fear makes me so unhappy! A mere nothing unnerves me, and the coward's flight barely saves him in time. But I must run: from my refuge I hear the sound of a horn or two!"

[2] But it was only the rustle of the wind, and the animal realized his mistake. Yet without a word he bounded into the fields, fearing that the hunter was right behind him. One may read, observe, and learn, but to no avail—fear has no cure.

[3] Our coward in his flight found even greater cowards: he passed by a marsh that harbored a group of frogs. This primitive folk suddenly leaped into the water to seek refuge.

[4] "I say, they're frightened when I pass by," said the runner. "What is this, then? Perhaps I should be a bit bolder. But I'm afraid I must have real courage as well, and our species, no matter what we do, will never have anything but a faint heart."

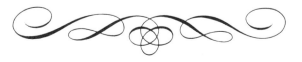

Les Grenouilles Qui Demandent un Roi

L'amour du changement

I Les gre- nouil- les se las- sant De l'é-tat dé- mo- cra- ti- que, Par leurs cla- meurs fi- rent tant Qu'on leur ren- dit mo- nar- chi- que. Nous vou- lons, nous vou- lons a- voir un roi, Di- sait

II Le pre- mier qu'on leur don- na Fut un man- che de cha- ru- e. Il fit peur quand il tom- ba, Et cha- cune en fit é- mu- e; Mais bien- tôt, mais bien- tôt le vo- yant coi, Il faut

la gent a - qua - ti - que, Nous vou - lons, nous vou - lons a - voir un roi, Qui nous
voir comme on le hu - e; Mais bien - tôt, mais bien - tôt le vo - yant coi, On de -

tien - ne sous sa loi.
mande un au - tre roi.

III

A la place du perclus
En vient un qui se remue,
Et qui vole, c'est bien plus:
En un mot, c'est une grue.
Et d'abord, et d'abord Sa Majesté
  Fait main basse, croque, tue;
Et d'abord, et d'abord Sa Majesté
  Fait haïr sa royauté.

IV

Et grenouilles de prier
Qu'on leur donne un autre sire:
Mais on les laissa crier,
Se contentant de leur dire:
Dépendez, dépendez de celui-là,
  De peur qu'il n'en vienne un pire,
Dépendez, dépendez de celui-là;
  Et l'affaire finit là.

THE FROGS WHO WANT TO HAVE A KING
Love of change

[1] The frogs, tired of living in a democracy, clamored so loud and so long, that finally a monarchy was proclaimed. "We want, we want a king," cried the watery folk, "who will keep us under his rule!"

[2] The first king they were given was a plow-handle. When he fell, all were frightened and upset. But soon, seeing that he never moved, everyone mocked him, and demanded a new king.

[3] The deposed monarch's place was taken by one who moved about quite well; what's more, he flew—in a word, it was a crane. And right away, His Majesty began to scoop up, kill and swallow, and made his regime hateful.

[4] So the frogs begged to be given another master; but their pleas were ignored. They were simply told that they must be satisfied with what they had, for fear that an even worse king might follow. And there the affair ended.

Les Deux Mulets
Faste dangereux

Léger

I Deux mu - lets fai - saient un vo - ya - ge, L'un char - gé d'or; L'au - tre de fruits de

II Au bruit qu'il fait de sa son - net - te, Vient le vo - leur: On cher - che l'or, et

ORIGINAL KEY: G

20

jar - di - na - ge, Ché - tif tré - sor. Le pre - mier d'une al - lu - re fiè - re Fai -
l'on se jet - te Sur le por - teur. Il se dé - fend; mais on l'ac - ca - ble De

sait le fat; Lais - sait son com - pa - gnon der - riè - re Comme un gou - jat.
mil - le coups. Gens fas - tu - eux, à cet - te fa - ble Que di - tes - vous?

III
L'autre mulet que nul n'arrête,
  Allait son pas;
Et secouant un peu la tête,
  Disait tout bas:
J'estime fort, cher camarade,
  Ton bel emploi;
Mais j'aime mieux porter salade;
  Tu vois pourquoi.

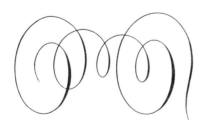

THE TWO MULES
Dangerous display

[1] Two mules were making a trip. One was loaded with gold; the other carried a lowly treasure: garden vegetables. The first strutted along ostentatiously and left his companion behind, as if he were unfit to be seen with.

[2] A thief heard the jingle of the proud mule's bell. Looking for gold, he attacked. The poor victim tried to defend himself, but he was overcome by countless blows. (You people who display your wealth, what say you to our fable?)

[3] The second mule, whom nothing threatened, slowed his pace. Shaking his head a little, he murmured, "My dear fellow, I realize that your task is a splendid one; but I'd rather carry greens—you can see why."

La Tortue
et les Deux Canards

Babil imprudent, et vaine curiosité

ORIGINAL KEY: D

I U - ne tor - tue, à la tê - te lé - gè - re, Veut vo - ya - ger, et cou - rir le pa - ys. Sots cu - ri - eux ai - ment terre é - tran - gè - re; Boi - teux ha - ïs - sent le lo - gis.

II Par deux ca - nards est faite u - ne ma - chi - ne. Cet - te ma - chine é - tait un long bâ - ton, Où par les dents te - nait la pè - le - ri - ne: Ser - rez bien fer - me, lui dit - on.

III
Les deux oiseaux la portent par les nues:
Tout s'ébahit, et l'on crie en tous lieux:
Ah! venez voir la reine des tortues
Dans le chemin qui mène aux cieux.

IV
Oui, je la suis, messieurs, ne vous déplaise,
Dit l'innocente, et lâche le bâton:
La dame tombe; on rit de sa fadaise:
Mais elle en pleure tout de bon.

THE TORTOISE AND THE TWO DUCKS
Imprudent chatter and vain curiosity

[1] A feather-brained tortoise desired to travel, and see the country. (Curious fools love foreign parts; cripples hate to stay home.)

[2] Two ducks hit upon an idea: they would carry a long stick which our pilgrim would grip between her teeth. "Hold on tightly!" they warned her.

[3] The two birds carried her up into the clouds. All who saw them cried out in astonishment, "Come and see the queen of the tortoises on her journey through the sky!"

[4] "Yes, that's who I am, may it please you, sirs," said the naive creature, letting go of the stick. Her Highness fell; they laughed at her stupidity; but she cried in earnest.

Les Deux Chèvres
Le point d'honneur

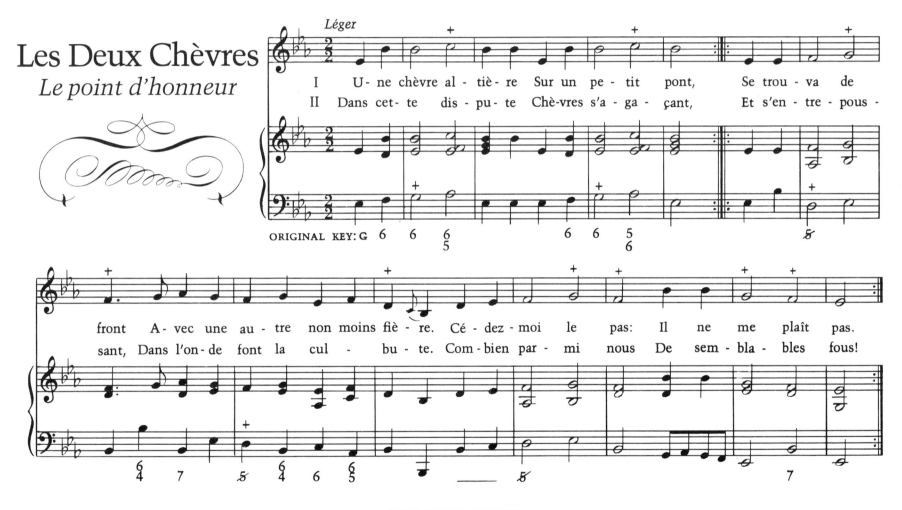

THE TWO GOATS
Point of honor

[1] A haughty goat crossing a narrow bridge came face to face with another goat, who was no less proud. "Make way for me!" (said one). "Suppose I don't want to?" (said the other).

[2] As they argued, their tempers flared; and, pushing and shoving, they both tumbled into the water. How many crazy fools like them exist among us!

Le Levraut et la Tortue

Hâtez-vous lentement

Marqué

I Qui ne part au point cer - tain, Court et ga - lope en vain.
II Ils a - vaient ga - gé tous deux Et mis de bons en jeux.

ORIGINAL KEY: A

Que l'on s'a - nime et s'é - ver - tu - e, Rien ne cor - ri - ge ce dé - faut: La tor -
Al - lez tou - jours, dit le com - pè - re, Il ne me faut que deux in - stants: La com -

tu - e Se rend plu - tôt Au but que le le - vraut.
mè - re Prend les de - vants Et ne perd pas de temps.

24

III

Le coureur la voit enfin
Presqu'au bout du chemin:
Comme un trait part de l'arbalète,
Il part, il vole, mais sans fruit;
    Et la bête,
   Dit-on, perdit
L'honneur et le profit.

THE HARE AND THE TORTOISE
Run slowly

[1] If you don't start in time, you'll hurry in vain. You may strive and strain, but nothing can alter that fact. The tortoise, remember, reached the goal sooner than the hare.

[2] The two of them made a bet and laid their money down for a race. "Go on ahead," said the hare, "it will only take me two seconds." So the tortoise lost no time in getting on her way.

[3] At last the racer noticed that the tortoise had almost reached the finish line. Swift as an arrow shot from a bow he flew, but to no avail. And so the animal lost both his honor and his bet.

L'Ours et les Deux Gascons

La peau d'ours

jours, Ils de-vaient é-cor-cher leur ours: Mais ce-lui-ci de son co-
pa, Au plus haut d'un chê-ne grim-pa. L'autre à cou-rir un peu moins

té Se mo-qua de ce beau trai-té.
fort, Se cou-chant, con-tre-fit le mort.

III

Autour de l'homme gisant,
Qui point ne bouge et ne respire,
Notre bête allait flairant,
Et sa grimace semblait dire:
Il faudra rompre le marché;
Point de peau, j'en suis bien fâché.
Quand vous voudrez la mettre à prix,
Attendez que vous m'ayez pris.

THE BEAR AND THE TWO GASCONS
Don't sell a bearskin until you've caught a bear

[1] There once were two braggarts who were out of money, so they decided that they would sell the skin of a wild bear they planned to trap. In two or three days, they thought, they'd have their bear all skinned. But the animal had his own opinion of their clever plans.

[2] So the two set out, confident of success. But as soon as the bear appeared, their hair stood on end. The quicker of the two escaped, and climbed to the top of a tree. The other one couldn't run fast enough, so he threw himself down and played dead.

[3] He lay there motionless, holding his breath; and as the bear sniffed around him, he seemed to say, "You'll have to forget your big sale, you'll get no skin today—I'm really annoyed! Before you decide what price you're going to ask, make sure that you've caught me!"

27

Le Rat de Ville et le Rat des Champs
La vie champêtre

I Le rat de ville au rat des champs Un soir faisait grand chè-
II A-dieu, dit le rat vil-la-geois Au ci-ta-din tout blê-

re, Mais un tris-te con-tre-temps Gâ-ta tou-te l'af-fai-re: Du lo-gis vien-nent les
me; Ja-mais au fond de nos bois Je ne trem-blai de mê-me: Je vous laisse a-vec vos

gens; Les chats ne tar-dent guè-re.
rois Et vo-tre peur ex-trê-me.

ORIGINAL KEY: G

THE CITY RAT AND THE COUNTRY RAT
Country living

[1] The city rat gave the country rat a sumptuous banquet one evening. But something happened that ruined the whole thing: people suddenly came out of the house, and the rats knew that the cats would be right behind them.

[2] "Goodbye!" the rustic said to the city-dweller, who was pale as a ghost. "Never have I had a fright like this down in my woods. I leave you to your kings—and to your fear and trembling!"

29

Le Loup Berger

Trompeur
pris dans son piège

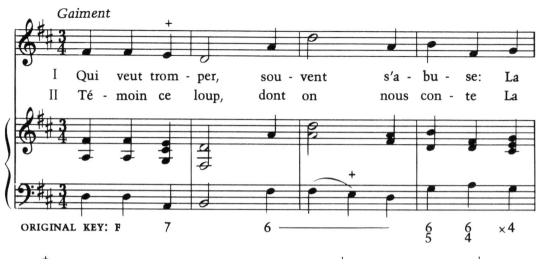

Gaiment

ORIGINAL KEY: F

I Qui veut trom - per, sou - vent s'a - bu - se: La
II Té - moin ce loup, dont on nous con - te La

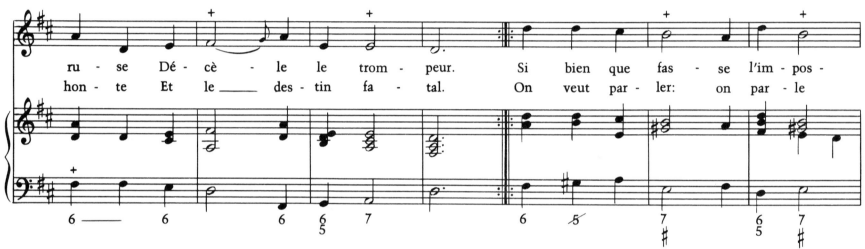

ru - se Dé - cè - le le trom - peur. Si bien que fas - se l'im - pos -
hon - te Et le _____ des - tin fa - tal. On veut par - ler: on par - le

III
En hoqueton ou souquenille
    Le drille
  Se fit voir au troupeau.
Contre la tige d'un ormeau
Se tenant droit comme une quille,
En hoqueton ou souquenille
    Le drille
  Se fit voir au troupeau.

IV
Il prétendait ainsi surprendre,
    Et prendre
  Bon nombre de brebis.
C'est pour cela qu'il avait mis
L'accoutrement qu'on vient d'entendre:
Il prétendait ainsi surprendre,
    Et prendre
  Bon nombre de brebis.

V
Le sot voulut comme Tityre
    Leur dire,
  Au pain, moutons, au pain.
Sachant déjà de longue main
Que c'est le mot qui les attire,
Le sot voulut comme Tityre
    Leur dire,
  Au pain, moutons, au pain!

VI
Il n'eût pas mal joué son rôle,
    Le drôle;
  On l'eût pris pour berger,
S'il avait su mieux ménager
L'air et le ton de la parole.
Il n'eût pas mal joué son rôle,
    Le drôle;
  On l'eût pris pour berger.

VII
Mais à sa voix, voix de furie,
    Tout crie,
  A la bête, au larron!
Sous les habits de Corydon
Il faisait bien la comédie;
Mais à sa voix, voix de furie,
    Tout crie,
  A la bête, au larron!

VIII
Et le vilain, quand on le brave,
    S'entrave
  Dans l'habit emprunté.
Jusqu'au mouton le plus crotté,
Pour l'assommer tout fait le brave.
Et le vilain, quand on le brave,
    S'entrave
  Dans l'habit emprunté.

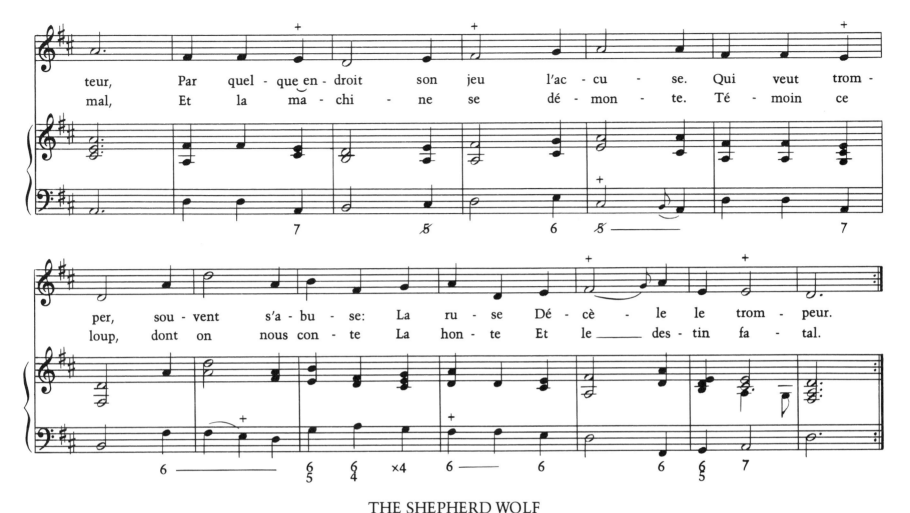

teur, Par quel- que_en- droit son jeu l'ac - cu - se. Qui veut trom -
mal, Et la ma- chi - ne se dé- mon - te. Té - moin ce

per, sou - vent s'a - bu - se: La ru - se Dé - cè - le le trom - peur.
loup, dont on nous con - te La hon - te Et le ___ des - tin fa - tal.

THE SHEPHERD WOLF
The trickster caught in his own trap

[1] A would-be deceiver is often foiled: the trickster is betrayed by his own ruse. No matter how skillful the imposter is, something will give him away. (A would-be deceiver is often fooled: the trickster is betrayed by his own ruse.)

[2] A good example of this is the wolf whose shame and unhappy end are told in this story. He tried to speak; he spoke badly, and his plan fell apart. (A good example of this is the wolf whose shame and unhappy end are told in this story.)

[3] Dressed in a tunic or shepherd's garb, the rascal showed himself to the flock. Against the trunk of an elm, he held himself straight as a bowling pin. (Dressed in a tunic or shepherd's garb, the rascal showed himself to the flock.)

[4] He counted on surprising and catching a fair number of lambs. That's why he wore the costume just described. (He counted on surprising and catching a fair number of lambs.)

[5] The fool planned to call, like Tithyrus the shepherd,

"Here's your food, sheep, come eat!" knowing well that these words would make them come. (The fool planned to call, like Tithyrus the shepherd, "Here's your food, sheep, come eat!")

[6] He wouldn't have played his role badly, the clown—they would have mistaken him for their shepherd, if he'd only known how to control the tone of his voice. (He wouldn't have played his role badly, the clown—they would have mistaken him for their shepherd.)

[7] But at the sound of his voice—a demon's voice—they all cried, "Wolf, thief!" In Corydon's clothes he played his part well. (But at the sound of his voice—a demon's voice—they all cried, "Wolf, thief!")

[8] And the rogue, as he was being chased, became entangled in his borrowed clothes. All the sheep, down to the mangiest among them, fearlessly attacked him. (And the rogue, as he was being chased, became entangled in his borrowed clothes.)

31

Le Loup
et la Cicogne

L'ingratitude des grands

Gaiment

I Man - geant à sa gui - se, Un loup grand glou -
II Pour un tel ser - vi - ce, Le plus grand de

ORIGINAL KEY: g

ton, Eut la gor - ge pri - se D'un os de mou -
tous, Dit l'o - pé - ra - tri - ce, Que me don - nez -

ton. Par bon - heur u - ne ci - go - gne Vint tout
vous? Ton sa - lai - re c'est ta vi - e, Ré - pon -

32

à pro - pos: Et s'é - tant mise en be -
dit le loup; Je ne te l'ai point ra -

so - gne, Lui ti - ra cet os.
vi - e: N'est - ce pas beau - coup?

III

Ton col sans dommage
De ma gueule sort;
Vouloir davantage
N'as-tu pas grand tort?
Quelqu'office qu'on nous rende,
A nous autres grands,
La récompense est trop grande
D'éviter nos dents.

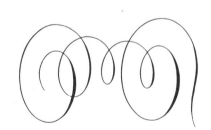

THE WOLF AND THE STORK
The ingratitude of the great

[1] A great glutton of a wolf was gobbling down his meal, when a lamb-bone became stuck in his throat. Fortunately a stork came along just then, and, setting to work, she pulled the bone out.

[2] "For such a service (there is none greater)," said the surgeon bird, "what will you give me?" "Your fee is this: your life," answered the wolf. "I didn't hurt you—isn't that enough?

[3] "Your neck left my throat unharmed; asking for more would be wrong, don't you think? Whatever you may do for us important people, merely escaping our teeth is too great a reward!"

La Fourmi et la Sauterelle
L'oisiveté

I Pen - dant l'é - té, Chante et bon - dit la sau - te - rel - le;
II Pen - dant l'hi - ver, La sau - te - relle est sans pi - tan - ce;

ORIGINAL KEY: G

Pen - dant l'é - té, On la voit dans l'oi - si - ve - té; Mais au tra - vail prompte
Pen - dant l'hi - ver, Elle est ré - duite à vi - vre d'air; Et la four - mi dans

et __ fi - dè - le, La four - mi ne fait pas comme el - le, Pen - dant l'é - té.
l'a - bon - dan - ce, Lui dit: bel - le chan - teu - se, dan - se, Pen - dant l'hi - ver.

THE ANT AND THE GRASSHOPPER
Sloth

[1] In summertime the grasshopper leaps and sings; in summertime she's always idle. But, unlike her, the ant promptly and steadily does her work in summertime.

[2] In wintertime the grasshopper has nothing to eat; in wintertime she's forced to live on air. And the ant, who now has plenty, tells her, "Dance, pretty songstress, in wintertime!"

L'Enfant et le Maître d'Ecole

Le pédant

Rondement et marqué

I Ha-ran-gue sur ha-ran-gue, Que sert tant de dis-cours? Pé-dant, bri-de ta lan-gue, Et viens à mon se-cours: Viens vite et me re-lè-ve, Di-sait un jeune é-lè-ve Prêt à pé-rir dans l'eau; Lors-que son pé-da-go-gue Lui fai-sait d'un ton ro-gue Ser-mon tou-jours nou-veau.

THE BOY AND THE SCHOOLMASTER
The pedant

"Words, words, words—what use is a sermon to me? You pedant, hold your tongue and give me a hand—quick, help me out of here!" cried a young scholar about to drown in a pond. And his teacher just stood there lecturing him severely.

Le Coq et le Renard
Fin contre fin

I Un coq en sen - ti - nel - le, Veil - lait a - vant le _____ jour, Quand un re - nard l'ap ma

II L'oi - seau qui n'est pas bê - te, Ré - pond, Je suis à _____ toi, J'en ju - re par ma

ORIGINAL KEY: a

36

pel - le, Pour lui jou - er d'un ___ tour: Di - sant, la paix est fai - te, Et l'a - mi -
crê - te: Mais qu'est - ce que je ___ vois? Deux chiens vers nô - tre gî - te Ac - cou - rent

tié par - fai - te: Tu me vois dé - pu - té, Pour fai - re le trai - té.
au plus vi - te; Et com - me po - stil - lons, Fran - chis - sent les sil - lons.

III

La paix est générale,
C'est ici le congrès.
Mais le renard détale,
Et gagne les guérets:
J'ai, dit-il, une affaire,
Je vais plutôt la faire;
Et je double le pas,
Pour ne la manquer pas.

IV

Le coq en rit, et chante
A poules et chapons,
L'aventure plaisante
Qu'ici nous racontons:
On entend la poulaille
Qui répète et criaille:
N'a pas petit honneur,
Qui trompe le trompeur.

THE COCK AND THE FOX
Battle of the wits

[1] A cock on guard duty was watching for dawn, when a fox called up to him, thinking he'd play a good trick. "Peace has been declared," he said, "and ours will be a perfect friendship. I'm here to draw up the treaty."

[2] The bird, who was no fool, replied, "I wholeheartedly accept, I swear it by my crest! But what's that I see?—two dogs racing towards our roost, leaping the furrows like courriers.

[3] "Why, it's a universal peace, and we're *all* meeting here!" But the fox scampered off to the fields. "I have an urgent appointment," he called, "that I really should keep; I must run, or I'll miss it!"

[4] The cock laughed, and crowed to the hens and capons the merry tale we've just told. You can hear the chickens crying to each other, "It's no small honor to deceive the deceiver!"

Le Renard et
le Loup

La dupe

Légèrement

ORIGINAL KEY: G

I Au fond d'un puits par a - ven - tu - re,
II Le pri - son - nier se prend à ri - re,

Se lais - sa choir Re - nard ma - tois. On ne va pas tou - jours d'u - ne
Et con - tre - fai - re le joy - eux. Le loup vient, le re - garde: Eh! com-

dé - mar - che su - re; Et Bu - cé - phale a bron - ché quel - que fois.
ment, mon bon si - re, Es - tu, dit - il, des - cen - du dans ces lieux?

III

Fort aisément, mon bon compère,
Répond Renard: fais comme moi.
Tu trouveras encore de quoi faire grand chère;
Vois ce fromage: il est de bon aloi.

IV

Met dans ce seau ta corpulence:
Il se rencontre heureusement
Avec un autre ici qui le contrebalance;
Et la voiture ira fort doucement.

V

Le sot entra dans la machine,
Et le rusé dans l'autre aussi.
L'un en bas, l'autre en haut
  en même temps chemine:
Et le rusé dit au sot, Grand merci.

VI

Mais qu'est-ce encore que ce fromage,
Qui du gourmand fut l'hameçon?
La lune qui peignait dans l'onde
  son image.
On nous séduit de semblable façon.

THE FOX AND THE WOLF
The dupe

[1] Once it happened that a sly fox fell down a well. (Nobody is sure-footed all the time; even Bucephalus stumbled now and then.)

[2] The prisoner began to laugh, and pretended to be having a great time. A wolf came and looked down at him. "Goodness me, dear fellow," he cried, "how did you get down there?"

[3] "Very easy, old chap," answered the fox. Do as I did: You'll find enough left here to make a nice meal. See this cheese? It's really first class!

[4] "Just stuff yourself into that bucket. Luckily there's another one here to balance your weight, so you'll have a smooth ride."

[5] The fool got into the bucket, and the crafty fox jumped into the other one. As one went down, the other went up, and the fox called out to his simple friend, "Many thanks!"

[6] And what was this cheese that served as bait for the glutton?—only the moon reflected in the water. We are seduced in just the same way.

La Lice et sa Compagne

L'ingratitude

ORIGINAL KEY: d

I La lice à sa voi-si-ne Se fit prê-ter ja-
II Tou-jours ex-cu-se prê-te Pour ne point dé-ma-

dis _____ Le lit et la chau-mi-ne Pour fai-re ses pe-
rer: _____ Re-quê-te sur re-quê-te, Aux fins de dif-fé-

tits. _____ Huit jours, dit la com-mè-re, Quinze au plus, c'est as-
rer. _____ At-ten-dez, di-sait-el-le, Que mes fai-bles en-

41

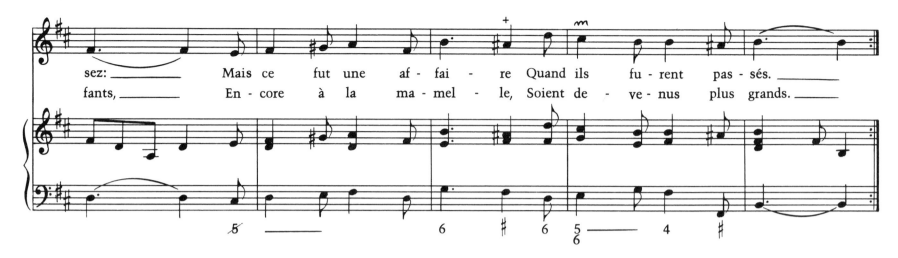

THE HOUND AND HER NEIGHBOR
Ingratitude

III

Mais quand la troupe forte
Peut garder la maison,
On parle d'autre sorte,
Sans rime ni raison.
Inutile semonce:
Matins restent dedans:
Et pour toute réponse,
Montrent de bonnes dents.

IV

Ce qu'aux méchants on prête
N'est pas toujours rendu:
En vain on le répète,
Ce n'est qu'un soin perdu.
D'abord on vous amuse,
Bientôt il faut plaider;
Et la force ou la ruse
Vous font enfin céder.

[1] Once upon a time a hound asked to borrow her neighbor's cottage so that she could give birth to her puppies in comfort. "A week or two at the most will be enough," she said. But when the time was up, the trouble began.

[2] She always found an excuse for not moving out. Each plea only resulted in a new postponement. "Just wait," she said, "until the feeble little pups are weaned, and have grown a bit."

[3] But when the mighty clan was able to guard the house, it was another story, without rhyme or reason. It was no use pleading; they were there to stay. And now their only answer was to bare their fine teeth.

[4] What is lent to ingrates is rarely returned. In vain you may ask—it's only wasted breath. At first it may amuse you, but soon you will have to beg: deceit or force will defeat you in the end.

Le Renard et les Raisins
Gasconnade

le Gas - con, Et qui dans la Nor - man - di - e Au - rait pu don - ner le - çon,
tant trop haut, Je se - rais, dit - il, bien gru - e D'es - say - er un au - tre saut:

Vit un jour sur u - ne treil - le Grap - pe d'ex - cel - lent rai - sin, Et dont la cou - leur ver -
Ce n'est que de la gue - nil - le, Franc ver - jus pour des gou - jats: Qu'un autre à son gré le

meil - le Pro - met - tait re - pas très fin.
pil - le, S'il lui plaît d'en fai - re cas.

THE FOX AND THE GRAPES
Big talk

[1] There once was a fox who had a streak of the Gascon* in him, and who could have taught a few lessons in Normandy. One day he spied a luscious bunch of grapes hanging in an arbor; their ripe ruby color promised a delightful treat.

[2] He tried a leap or two, but the prize was too high. "I'd be a fool to try again," he said. "They're not worth the effort anyway—they're obviously sour, only a dolt would want them. If someone else wants to bother, he's welcome to try."

*Gascons were known as big talkers, who liked to stretch facts for their own convenience.

43

Le Singe Adopté
Le naturel

I De la gent ma - go - te Sot - te - ment é - pris, Un

II Voi - là Mon-sieur Sin - ge Pa - ré ri - che - ment: Beau

homme à ma - rot - te N'a - yant point de fils, Se mit dans la tê - te D'a -

drap, et beau lin - ge, Plus beau di - a - mant, Per - ru - que bien blon - de, Plu -

dop - ter Ber - trand, Et fit de la bê - te Son u - nique en - fant.

met au cha - peau An - non - cent au mon - de L'A - do - nis nou - veau.

ORIGINAL KEY: G

45

III

Il a pédagogues
De toutes façons,
Savants dialogues,
Savantes leçons.
On est à lui faire
Prendre tous les plis,
Qu'un millionaire
Fait prendre à son fils.

V

Que sert la tournure,
Et l'air et l'habit?
Jamais la nature
Ne se contredit.
La métamorphose
Du tempérament
N'est pas une chose
Qu'on fasse aisément.

IV

Enfin avec l'âge
On devient majeur:
Bertrand hors de page
Et sans gouverneur
Dérange, chiffonne,
Grimpe sur les toits,
Magot en personne
Tout comme autrefois.

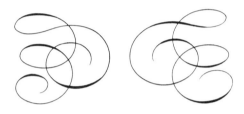

THE ADOPTED MONKEY
When nature takes its course

[1] There once was a man who loved monkeys to the point of absurdity. Being childless, he took it into his head to adopt Bertie as his only son.

[2] Now just look at Little Lord Monkey in his fine attire: expensive suits and fine linen shirts, sparkling diamonds, a silky blond wig, and a feather in his cap. All this presents the world with a new Adonis.

[3] He had every conceivable kind of tutor, intellectual discussions, and philosophy lessons. No effort was spared to teach him all that a millionaire's son should know.

[4] And in time he came of age. His schooling finished, restrained no longer, Bertie lost all control. Climbing about on the rooftops, he was the same old monkey as before.

[5] What good were the education, the manners he'd learned, the fancy dress? Mother Nature never contradicts herself. To transform someone's character is anything but easy.

Les Deux Chiens
L'inclination

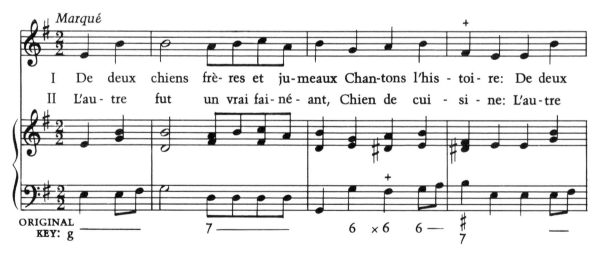

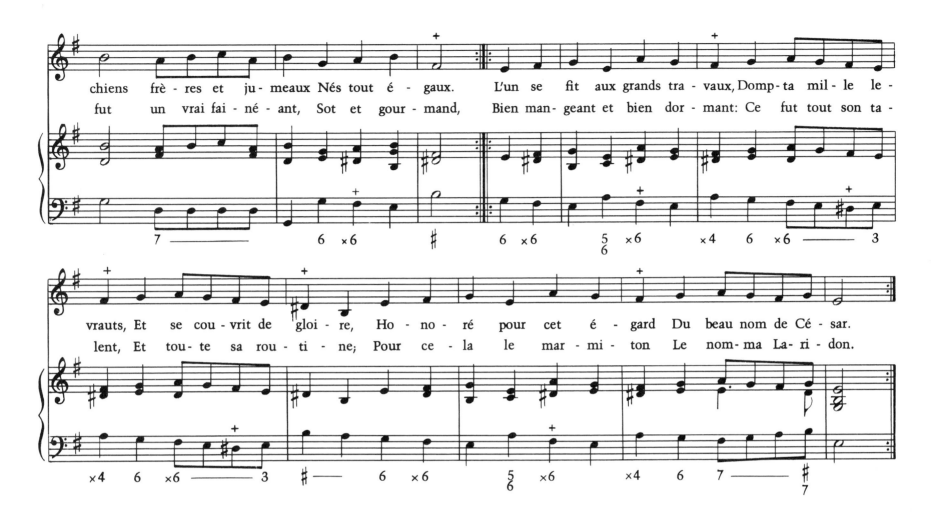

chiens frè - res et ju - meaux Nés tout é - gaux. L'un se fit aux grands tra - vaux, Domp - ta mil - le le -

fut un vrai fai - né - ant, Sot et gour - mand, Bien man - geant et bien dor - mant: Ce fut tout son ta -

vrauts, Et se cou - vrit de gloi - re, Ho - no - ré pour cet é - gard Du beau nom de Cé - sar.

lent, Et tou - te sa rou - ti - ne; Pour ce - la le mar - mi - ton Le nom - ma La - ri - don.

III

Parmi nous, voire chez les rois,
  C'est tout de même:
Parmi nous, voire chez les rois,
  Souventes fois
De deux frères que j'y vois,
  L'un par de beaux exploits
  Acquiert honneur suprème;
  L'autre à rien ne paraît bon,
  Et n'est qu'un laridon.

THE TWO DOGS
Inclination

[1] Here is the story of two dogs, twin brothers, exactly alike when they were born. One of them exerted himself to the utmost, caught hundreds of rabbits, and covered himself with glory. For this he was rewarded with the fine name "Caesar."

[2] His brother was good for nothing: just a kitchen-dog, a lazy glutton. His talents were sleeping and eating, and that's all he ever did. And so the kitchen boy named him "Lazybones."

[3] Amongst us, even in the king's court, it's the same story. More than once I've seen brothers like that. The brilliant achievements of one earn him the highest honors; the other is never good at anything—he's just a lazybones.

La Mouche et le Coche

Vain empressement

Rondement et marqué

I Dans un a - mas d'é - pais - se bou - e É - tait un char bien- a - vant en - ga - gé; L'es - sieu plon - geait a - vec la rou - e, Et le char - ton cri - ait en en - ra - gé, Quand là - des - sus u - ne mou - che s'ap - pro - che; Fai - sons al - ler ce

II Ces che - veaux- là sont des ma - zet - tes, Pour - sui - vit- elle, et de son ai - guil - lon Pi - quait plus vif que des mo - let - tes, Tan - tôt au flanc et tan - tôt au chi - gnon: El - le par - lait en mal de l'at - ta - la - ge, Pour fai - re da - van-

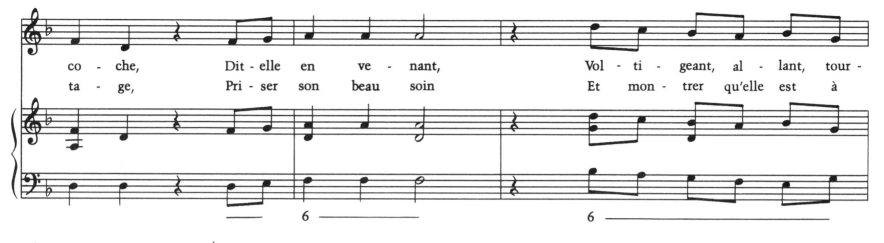

co - che, Dit - elle en ve - nant,   Vol - ti - geant, al - lant, tour -
ta - ge, Pri - ser son beau soin   Et mon - trer qu'elle est à

nant, Tou - jours bour - don - nant.
point Ve - nue au be - soin.

III

Enfin on se tire d'affaire:
L'impertinente en prétend tout l'honneur;
Elle veut encore un salaire,
Argent comptant pour son fameux labeur.
O qu'il en est de cette espèce vaine
    Parmi la race humaine!
    Gens à s'empresser,
  Gens à s'embarrasser;
    Gens bons à chasser.

THE FLY AND THE COACH
Unnecessary zeal

[1] In a deep mud-hole a coach was deeply mired. The wheels were in up to the axle, and the driver bellowed furiously. Then along came a fly. "Let's get this thing moving," she said, circling back and forth with a steady buzz.

[2] "These horses are old worn-out nags," she added, and with a sting sharper than spurs she took aim at their flanks and backs. She cursed at the team so that her own great efforts would shine, and make it seem that she'd arrived in the nick of time.

[3] Finally the coach was freed. The impertinent little creature claimed all the credit, and what's more she expected a reward: cash on the line for her self-proclaimed labors. How many such vain creatures there are among humans—people who urge, people who annoy, people who should be driven away.

La Besace
L'amour propre

Légèrement

I Cha - cun   a   ses a - van - ta - ges, Et cha - cun   a   ses dé -   fauts:

II Ja - dis dans   leur as - sem - blé - e, (Car ja - dis   il s'en fai -   sait)

ORIGINAL KEY: d   7   5 ——   6   ×6   ×6   7

50

Mais par - mi les a - ni - maux Do - me - sti - ques et sau - va - ges, Cha - cun
Le ma - got s'ap-plau - dis - sait De sa tê - te bien mou - lé - e; Et sur

croit ê - tre le mieux, Et vou - drait tous les hom - ma - ges: Cha - cun
l'ours, qu'il hon - nis - sait, Fai - sait fai - re la hu - é - e: Et sur

croit ê - tre le mieux, Et lui seul plaît à ses yeux.
l'ours, qu'il hon - nis - sait, Comme un ar - le - quin glo - sait.

III

L'ours très content de sa forme
Fit la moue à l'éléphant,
Disant qu'il était trop grand,
Et sa masse trop informe.
L'éléphant de son côté
Ne veut point qu'on le réforme:
L'éléphant de son côté
Dit mainte autre pauvreté.

IV

Monstrueuse est la baleine;
La fourmi n'est qu'un fétu,
N'est-ce pas? Qu'en penses-tu?
Dit-il à l'espèce humaine.
Celle-ci méprisa tout,
Se donnant louange pleine:
Celle-ci méprisa tout,
Seule parfaite à son gout.

V

Nous portons tous la besace
Qu'amour propre nous donna.
Tout mortel arrange là
Les défauts de chaque classe:
Par-devant sont ceux d'autrui,
Et les siens à l'autre place;
Par-devant sont ceux d'autrui,
Et les siens derrière lui.

THE BEGGAR'S DOUBLE SACK
Self-esteem

[1] Everyone has his good points, and everyone has his faults; but among the animals (both domestic and wild), each one thinks himself the best, and expects to have all the praise. Each one thinks himself the best, and only he is pleasing to his eyes.

[2] At one of their general meetings (for such they had once upon a time), the monkey was boasting of his head's exquisite shape. He heaped ridicule on the bear, and described him as a clown.

[3] The bear, quite content with the way he looked, turned up his nose at the elephant, saying that he was just too large, and quite shapeless, too. As for the elephant, he was not at all anxious to be changed. He in turn had some nasty things to say.

[4] "The whale is a monster, the ant's just a piece of straw, don't you agree? What's your opinion?" he asked a human being. This creature sneered at all the animals, giving himself all the glory. In his opinion, only he was perfect.

[5] All of us carry the beggar's sack which self-love has given us. In it each mortal arranges the various kinds of defects: in front he keeps those of other people; his own he carries in the other part, behind him.

Les Deux Chiens

Elaborated version

For an English translation of the lyrics, refer to p. 46.

(RECORDER TACET)

I *f* De deux chiens frè - res et ju-meaux Chan-tons l'his - toi - re: De deux chiens frè - res et ju -

II *p* L'au - tre fut un vrai fai - né - ant, Chien de cui - si - ne: L'au - tre fut un vrai fai - né -

f - p

meaux nés tout é - gaux ____. L'un se fit aux grands tra - vaux, Domp-ta mil - le le -
ant, Sot et gour - mand ____, Bien man - geant et bien dor - mant:_ Ce fut tout son ta -

vrauts,_ Et se cou-vrit de gloi - re, Ho - no - ré par cet é - gard_ Du beau nom de Cé -
lent,_ Et tou-te sa rou-ti - ne; Pour ce-la le mar - mi - ton_ Le nom-ma La-ri -

sar.   don.   3. Par - mi nous,   voi - re chez les

Rois, C'est tout de mê____me: Par - mi nous,   voi - re chez les Rois, Sou - ven - tes

fois _____ De deux frè - res que j'y vois, L'un par de beaux ex-ploits_ Ac - quiert hon-neur su-

prè - me; L'Au - tre à rien ne pa - raît bon, Et n'est qu'un la - ri - don _____.